NOT SO GREAT GUY FAWKES

Penny for the guy, Mister!

RICHARD BRASSEY

Orion
Children's Books

Who do you think of when you hear about gunpowder, treason and plot?

Who do you ask passers-by to give you a penny for?

Who do you remember, remember on the fifth of November?

Who do people burn every year on a bonfire?

GUY FAWKES

Guy was born in York in 1570. He had two younger sisters. Their father worked as an official in the courts and was a Protestant. Their mother was a Roman Catholic. In those days, whether you were Protestant or Catholic was a big deal.

Guy grew up in the time of Queen Elizabeth I. Her father, Henry VIII, had said the Pope wasn't head of the Church of England any more and made himself head instead. This turned England into a Protestant country, and caused lots of problems. The Spanish Armada even tried to invade and make England Catholic again.

Catholics in England had to pretend they weren't Catholic. Otherwise, they were seen as traitors who supported the Spanish enemy. Catholic priests were arrested if they were caught, so secret Catholics with big houses built hiding places for them known as 'priest holes'.

Guy spent a lot of his childhood at his Protestant grandmother's home. But when she died, all she left him was a whistle and a gold coin. His father died when he was eight and his mother got married again, this time to a Catholic.

Tell us where they are hidden!

Even if you squash me to death I won't tell you.

Guy went to St Peter's School, which still exists today. The headmaster and teachers were secret Catholics. The aunt of his best friend, Kit Wright, had been squashed to death for hiding two priests in her house.

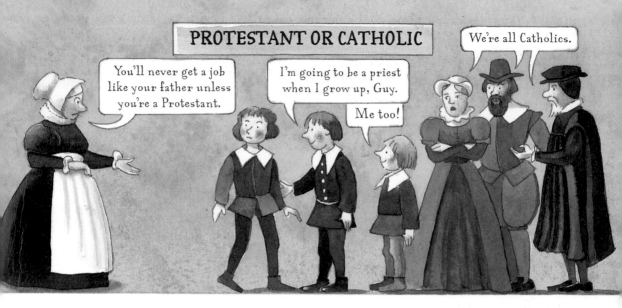

Indeed, most of his schoolfriends were Catholic. Several even became priests. But Guy's decision to be Catholic himself would make his life very difficult. Protestants ran everything in England and had all the best jobs.

He did manage to get a job when he was about twenty. He left York for Sussex to become a footman to Lord Montague, who was a secret Catholic. Unfortunately, for some reason Lord Montague didn't like him and soon fired him.

In 1603, Queen Elizabeth died and was succeeded by King James of Scotland, whose mother and wife were Catholic. Most Catholics were thrilled because they thought he'd promised they wouldn't have to keep their religion secret any more.

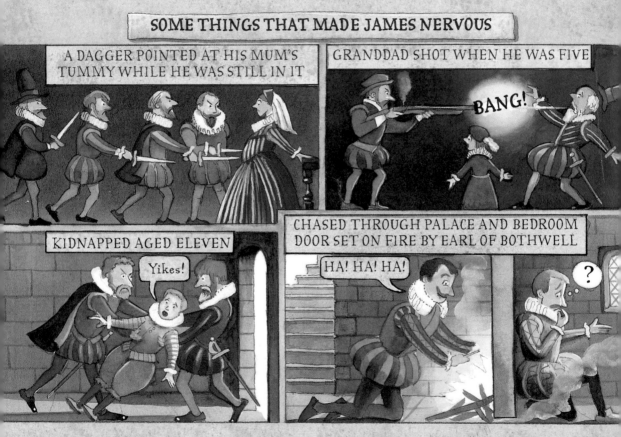

SOME THINGS THAT MADE JAMES NERVOUS

A DAGGER POINTED AT HIS MUM'S TUMMY WHILE HE WAS STILL IN IT

GRANDDAD SHOT WHEN HE WAS FIVE

BANG!

KIDNAPPED AGED ELEVEN

Yikes!

CHASED THROUGH PALACE AND BEDROOM DOOR SET ON FIRE BY EARL OF BOTHWELL

HA! HA! HA!

?

But James was nervous. When he arrived in England, he discovered some Catholics were plotting to get rid of him. He went back on his promises, ordered all priests to leave the country and fined anybody who didn't go to a Protestant church. Even his wife had to watch her step.

In the meantime, Guy had joined the Spanish army fighting Protestants in Flanders. He was a good soldier and became a captain. He began calling himself by the Spanish 'Guido' and he probably also learnt how to set fuses and blow things up with gunpowder during this time.

After James went back on his word, Guy travelled to Spain to ask them to try to invade England again. He didn't realise Spain couldn't be bothered to fight England any more. When he got back to Flanders, a man called Tom Wintour came looking for him. Tom persuaded Guy to sail back to England with him.

In May 1604, five men met in a room at the Duck & Drake Inn on the Strand, London. They had been called together by Tom Wintour's cousin, Robert Catesby. Catesby told them he had a plan to blow up Parliament with the King and all the government inside and make England Catholic again.

ROBERT CATESBY

TOM WINTOUR

JACK WRIGHT
[brother of Kit, Guy's best friend at school]

The nature of the disease requires so sharp a remedy.

THOMAS PERCY

GUIDO FAWKES

Shall we always, gentlemen, talk and never do anything?

Afterwards they all swore an oath of secrecy on a prayer book. Then they went next door where a priest friend of theirs celebrated a secret mass.

Shhh! Don't tell Father Gerrard anything about it.

It seems odd now but the plotters were able to rent a flat bang next door to Parliament. Guy moved in under the false name of John Johnson to avoid suspicion. Nobody would recognise him because he'd been abroad so long.

PLOTTERS' HOUSE

HOUSE OF LORDS

TUNNEL

CELLAR

One story says they began to dig a tunnel but ran into a thick wall. There was no need. They found they could rent the cellar directly underneath the House of Lords where the King would open Parliament!

HOUSE OF COMMONS

Guy and the others set about rowing thirty-six barrels of gunpowder over from Catesby's house across the Thames. They piled them into the cellar and hid them under bundles of firewood. Everything was ready.

CATESBY'S HOUSE

RIVER THAMES

Then at the beginning of 1605, Parliament was delayed till autumn because of the plague in London. Guy went to Flanders in a last effort to get help from his friends in the Spanish army. James's chief minister, Sir Robert Cecil, had spies everywhere. He heard what Guy was up to in Flanders but it's unlikely he knew that Guy was also 'John Johnson'.

Will you help us?

Pensaré de él.

INSTRUCTIONS FOR MAKING GUNPOWDER

MIX TOGETHER: SULPHUR, CHARCOAL AND SALTPETRE WITH WATER

ALLOW TO DRY

USE BEFORE SELL-BY DATE

IF LEFT TOO LONG, IT WON'T EXPLODE ANY MORE. REMIX – **VERY DANGEROUS!**

When Guy got back to London, he realised the gunpowder was past its sell-by date. All thirty-six barrels had to be replaced.

It wasn't until October that the plotters, now including Guy's schoolfriend, Kit, decided the final details. Guy would light the fuse and escape across the Thames. Meanwhile, some of the others would ride to the Midlands, kidnap James's nine-year-old daughter Elizabeth, and make her a puppet queen.

We should be able to boss a nine-year-old girl around!

Psst! Give this letter to your master.

Then on 26th October 1605 an odd thing happened. The story goes that, as darkness fell, a passing stranger gave a letter to the servant of Lord Monteagle. The letter advised Monteagle not to go to Parliament.

Who wrote the letter is a big mystery to this day. But although Monteagle was a Catholic and was married to the sister of one of the plotters, he took the letter straight to Sir Robert Cecil. We can only guess that he thought that if the King was blown up, it would get all Catholics into much worse trouble than they were already in.

My Lord,
I would advise you, as you tender your life, to devise some excuse to shift your attendance at this Parliament . . .
They shall receive a terrible blow . . .
The danger is past as soon as you have burnt the letter.

Somebody's plotting to blow me up!

Brilliant, Sire!

Sir Robert didn't bat an eyelid. Had his spies already told him about the plot? He didn't even show the letter to the King until a few days later. He told James he hadn't a clue what it meant. James worked out all by himself that somebody must be plotting to blow him up.

So the day before the opening of Parliament, the Lord Chamberlain and Lord Monteagle pretended to take a stroll around the Parliament building. They noticed an awful lot of firewood in the cellar and a tall suspicious-looking man lurking by the cellar door.

At midnight a proper search party set off. The same tall man was still lurking. They immediately arrested him. In his pockets were a watch, some kindling and a box of matches. He said his name was Johnson. In the cellar, under all the firewood, they found the thirty-six barrels of gunpowder!

News of Guy's arrest quickly spread. Kit heard and raced round to the Duck &
Drake to warn Tom Wintour. The plotters all jumped on their horses and fled
north from London as fast as they could ride.

Guards were set on the city gates, but too late. All was chaos and rumour . . .
The King had been saved. Bonfires were lit to celebrate. Some said the Spanish
were behind the plot. An angry mob besieged the Spanish Ambassador's house.

Strange as it seems nowadays, Guy was immediately taken to the King's bedroom, where James demanded the names of the other plotters. Guy wouldn't tell. A letter addressed to 'Guy Fawkes' had been found in his pocket but he still claimed his name was John Johnson.

How could you plot to blow up me and my children?

A dangerous disease requires a desperate remedy!

Try the gentler tortures first.

He'll be a good foot longer by the time I'm finished!

James ordered him to be taken to the Tower of London. He was probably stretched on the rack and surprised everyone by how long he held out. It was three days before he named names. He can't have felt too good after all the torture. The signature on his confession looks very wonky.

Meanwhile the other plotters, just one step ahead of the law, arrived at Holbeach House, Staffordshire, during a rainstorm. They'd collected lots of gunpowder, which was soaked, so they spread it in front of the fire to dry . . . DUH! They got their explosion all right . . . but not the one they'd expected!

BOOM!

Stand by me and we will die together . . . Aargh!

The next day, two hundred government men caught up with them. In the shootout, Catesby and Percy were killed by the same bullet. The Wright brothers were also shot. Tom Wintour and three others were dragged back to London in chains. Catesby's and Percy's heads were chopped off to be displayed on the roof at Westminster.

In January, the trial of the surviving plotters took place in Westminster Hall. Catesby, the leader, was dead but Guy had been the one caught red-handed with the matches. It was Guy everybody wanted to see. All were found guilty of high treason and condemned to be hanged, drawn and quartered.

James watched unseen from a secret room. Throughout the trial the plotters had sat smoking their pipes, which must have upset him no end. He hated smoking almost as much as he hated the idea of being blown up.

Four days later, the crowds turned out to jeer as Guy and Tom were dragged on hurdles through the streets from the Tower to Westminster.

Guy was the last to be hanged. He was so weak from torture that the hangman had to help him climb the scaffold. He said little but asked the King to forgive him. Then he crossed himself, as Catholics do, which outraged the Protestant onlookers.

The noose broke his neck, killing him instantly. This was a huge disappointment to the crowd, who had hoped to see him cut down and then chopped into little bits while still alive . . . the usual punishment for high treason in those days.

I beg King James to forgive me.

He's dying in the very place which he planned to demolish.

Oh YUCK! He's crossing himself!

He's the greatest devil of all.

In the meantime, a hunt began for the three Catholic priests who were friends of the plotters. They hid where they could. When one emerged starving from a week in a priest hole, he looked such a sight that the searchers thought he was a ghost and at first ran away.

He was hanged. The two others escaped to the Continent, one of them hidden in a cargo of pigs.

The poor priests were blamed for the plot even though they probably hadn't wanted it in the first place. They knew the problems it would bring.

The Gunpowder Plot brought Catholics terrible trouble for centuries to come. New laws were passed to stop them being lawyers or officers in the Army or Navy. They couldn't live in London. They couldn't vote. They had trouble finding places to be buried unless they had joined the Church of England.

Plots were all anybody could talk about. Even Shakespeare wrote about a plot and a king's murder in his latest play, *Macbeth*.

Ever since, on the night before the opening of Parliament, the cellars have been searched by the Yeomen of the Guard in case somebody is plotting to blow up the monarch.

It became the custom for children to make a figure called a Guy from old clothes stuffed with newspaper or straw and beg passers-by for money to buy fireworks.

Bonfires have been lit ever since that first 5th of November in 1605. People often used to burn an effigy of the Pope but the figure who is usually on top of the fire is the one plotter everybody remembers . . . Guy Fawkes.